Best of Graphis
POSTER

PAGE ONE PUBLISHING

In the case of some of the reproductions in this book it proved impossible to locate the originals, despite careful research. They were, however, considered to be of such importance that the decision was taken by the present publisher to reproduce from other published sources.

Cover: *Self promotion poster,* Mendell + Oberer

© 1993 by Graphis Press Corp., Dufourstrasse 107, CH-8008 Zürich, Switzerland

© 1993 for this edition by Page One Publishing Pte Ltd., Singapore
Distributed worldwide by Könemann Verlagsgesellschaft mbH, Bonner Str. 126, D-50968 Köln

Designed by Peter Feierabend, Berlin
Text: Rolf Toman, Cologne
English translation: Michael Hulse, Cologne
French translation: Michèle Schreyer, Cologne

Printed in Singapore
ISBN 981-00-4766-5

Foreword

Since the mid-19th century, many countries in Europe and elsewhere have had columns in the anonymous metropolitan centres of modern life. Communications of various kinds are posted on these columns. Originally the size and conspicuousness of the notices and advertisements stuck on them were suited to the pace of passers-by. They evolved into posters once people began to pass by faster, using public and private transport. With the arrival of the automobile age, old-fashioned columns have been largely displaced from the cities that once had them, by immense billboards and hoardings.

A poster is a large graphic work that uses generous and often simplistic forms of expression to capture attention, in order to convey information or advertise. At times the print run has been included when defining a lithograph as a poster, and thus Honoré Daumier's 1864 "Charbon d'Ivory", the first mass-printed work of this kind, marks the beginning of poster history. I consider this criterion secondary, though, to the others. In 1963 Raymond Savignac, the great French poster designer, said of the poster that "any and every means to its objective are legitimate: emotion, wit, deception, blackmail, cynicism. The poster bears the same relation to the fine arts as freestyle wrestling does to good manners." With certain reservations (mainly in regard to various Japanese posters) we can agree with this. What interest me here are the fundamental characteristics of the poster, which remain, despite stylistic changes and cultural differences,. relatively constant.

The design parameters of posters are connected to the conditions in which people see them. If people are passing by hastily, the formal idiom must be clear, reduced to the essentials of the message. A good example is the poster for the 1986 Kiel Regatta on p. 30. It shows a white piece of paper, cut and torn to the shape of a sail, on a blue ground. For us to see this shape as a sail naturally pre-supposes our knowledge that the Kieler Woche (literally: Kiel Week) announced in the lettering is a boating event (and not, say, a paper trade fair). An even more pared-down poster, which dispenses entirely with words, is on p. 46. It shows two cigarettes placed cruciform, one burning to symbolize the deadly habit of smoking. Again, of course, we need to read the cross as a symbol of death to grasp the message. But this is so fundamental and universal that words become unnecessary.

Posters make their impact first and foremost through their visual qualities. Text reduced to a minimum tends to have an ancillary, reinforcing function. The typographical design, lettering placement and image are closely related, as the Malevich exhibition poster on p. 65 nicely shows. To my mind, the greatest aesthetic appeal of this poster lies in its successful minimalism and its extreme concentration on the message it was designed to convey.

Vorwort

Seit Mitte des 19. Jahrhunderts finden wir in den westlichen Metropolen, den Zentren anonymen öffentlichen Lebens, die Litfaßsäule als Träger graphischer Kommunikationsmittel. Die dort angeklebten Bekanntmachungen und Werbeblätter korrespondierten in ihrer Größe und Auffälligkeit anfangs noch mit dem Bewegungstempo und -radius des Fußgängers. Zu Plakaten wurden sie, als sich die Fortbewegung der Passanten durch die Benutzung öffentlicher und privater Verkehrsmittel zunehmend beschleunigte. Bedingt durch die gewaltig gewachsene Zahl der schnellen Automobilisten wurde die Litfaßsäule inzwischen weitgehend aus dem Stadtbild verdrängt und durch riesige Plakatwände ersetzt.

Das Plakat ist eine großflächige graphische Arbeit, die mit großzügigen Formen, oft von vereinfachendem Ausdruck, die Aufmerksamkeit des Betrachters auf sich zieht, um eine Sache bekanntzumachen und für sie zu werben. Man hat gelegentlich auch die Auflagenhöhe mit zur charakteristischen Bestimmung einer Lithographie als Plakat gezählt und im Hinblick darauf die Geschichte des Plakates mit Honoré Daumiers 1864 erstmals massenhaft gedruckten „Charbon d'Ivory" beginnen lassen. – Ich halte diesen Aspekt gegenüber den oben genannten für nachrangig. Raymond Savignac, der große französische Plakatentwerfer, sagte 1963 über das Plakat: „Alle Mittel sind ihm recht, um sein Ziel zu erreichen: Gefühl, Scherz, Täuschung, Erpressung, Zynismus ..., alles außer schamhafter Zurückhaltung. Zu den schönen Künsten steht das Plakat etwa im selben Verhältnis wie das Freistilringen zu guten Manieren." Mit gewissen Einschränkungen, die sich hauptsächlich auf zahlreiche japanische Plakate beziehen, kann man dieser Charakterisierung zustimmen. Mich interessieren im folgenden die grundsätzlichen Merkmale des Plakates, die bei allem stilistischen Wandel und bei aller kulturellen Differenz relativ konstant sind.

Die gestalterischen Voraussetzungen für Plakate hängen mit den Bedingungen zusammen, unter denen sie wahrgenommen werden. Das Flüchtige der Passanten verlangt eine klare, aufs Wesentliche der Botschaft reduzierte Formensprache. Ein sehr schönes Beispiel dafür finden wir in dem Plakat für die Kieler Woche 1986 auf Seite 30: ein in Segelform geschnittenes bzw. gerissenes weißes Blatt Papier auf blauem Hintergrund. Daß diese Form als Segel begriffen wird, dazu bedarf es freilich auch des Wissens des Betrachters, daß die Kieler Woche, die auf dem Plakat terminlich angekündigt wird, mit Wassersport (und nichts mit einer Fachmesse für Papier) zu tun hat. Ein noch weiter reduziertes, da ganz auf Text verzichtendes Plakat ist das auf Seite 46. Es zeigt zwei in Kreuzform übereinandergelegte Zigaretten, von denen die eine brennt, um damit die tödliche Gewohnheit des Rauchens zu thematisieren. Auch hier ist zum Verständnis der Botschaft wieder Hintergrundwissen vorausgesetzt: es bezieht sich auf das Kreuz als Zeichen des Todes. Dieses ist jedoch so elementar und allgemein, daß sich jeder textliche Hinweis erübrigt.

Plakate wirken in erster Linie kraft ihrer visuellen Botschaften. Der auf ein Minimum begrenzte Text hat eher ergänzende und unterstützende Funktion. Formal sind Typographie, das Schriftbild und Abbildung eng aufeinander bezogen, wie idealtypisch das Beispiel des Malewitsch-Ausstellungsplakates auf Seite 65 zeigt. Der größte ästhetische Reiz eines Plakates liegt für mich in der gelingenden Reduktion und der maximalen Konzentration seiner Elemente auf die Botschaft, für die es entworfen wurde.

Préface

Les colonnes d'affichage sont apparues dans les métropoles occidentales, centres d'une vie publique anonyme, vers le milieu du 19ème siècle. A l'origine, les avis et publicités qui y étaient collés correspondaient de par leur taille et leur aspect à la vitesse de déplacement des piétons et à leur rayon d'action. Ils se transformèrent en affiches quand les passants commencèrent à utiliser des moyens de transports publics et privés, et donc à être plus mobiles. Aujourd'hui, à cause du nombre croissant d'automobilistes rapides, la colonne Morris a quitté la ville et a été remplacée par de gigantesques panneaux d'affichage.

L'affiche est une feuille imprimée de grand format dont les formes généreuses et les expressions sobres attirent l'attention du spectateur pour lui faire connaître quelque chose et en faire la publicité. On a parfois aussi compté l'importance du tirage au nombre des critères faisant d'une lithographie une affiche et, en considération de cela, on a fait commencer l'histoire de l'affiche par la lithographie «Charbon d'Ivory» d'Honoré Daumier, imprimée en masse pour la première fois en 1864. Il me semble que cet aspect est secondaire. Raymond Savignac, le grand affichiste français, disait en 1963 à propos de l'affiche: «Tous les moyens lui sont bons pour atteindre son but: sentiment, plaisanterie, tromperie, chantage, cynisme... tout sauf une ré-serve pudique. L'affiche est aux Beaux-Arts à peu près ce que la lutte libre est aux bonnes manières.» Avec certaines réserves qui concernent surtout de nombreuses affiches japonaises, on peut approuver cette définition. Tournons-nous maintenant vers les caractères fondamentaux de l'affiche qui restent relativement constants à travers les styles et les particularités culturelles.

La forme de l'affiche est en rapport avec les conditions selon lesquelles elle est perçue. La mobilité fugitive des passants demande des formes claires réduisant le message à l'essentiel. Un très bel exemple en est l'affiche imprimée à l'occasion de la Kieler Woche en 1986 (page 30): un morceau de papier blanc découpé ou déchiré en forme de voile de bateau sur un fond bleu. Pour que cette forme soit perçue comme une voile il faut évidemment que l'observateur sache que la Kieler Woche an-noncée est en relation avec des sports nautiques (et non avec un Salon du papier). Une affiche encore plus réduite, puisqu'elle renonce complètement au texte se trouve page 46. Elle montre deux cigarettes en croix, dont l'une brûle, présentant ainsi l'habitude fatale du fumeur. Ici aussi un savoir sous-jacent, la croix symbole de mort, est nécessaire à la compréhension du message. Mais ce savoir est si général et élémentaire, que les mots sont superflus.

L'effet des affiches repose avant tout sur leurs messages visuels. Le texte réduit à un minimum a plutôt une fonction complémen-taire et de soutien. Au niveau de la forme la typographie, l'œil, et l'illustration se réfèrent étroitement l'un à l'autre, ce que montre par exemple de manière idéale l'affiche concernant l'exposition Malevitch page 65. Pour moi, le plus grand charme d'une affiche réside dans sa réduction réussie et la concentration maximum de ses éléments sur le message pour lequel elle a été conçue.

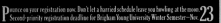

Designer
Heinz Edelmann
Description
Posters for theatre

Designer
McRay Magleby
Description
University registration deadline posters

Art Director
Timothy L. Eaton
Designers
T. Eaton P. Swenson and
B. Pederson
Photographer
Paul Shambroom
Description
Poster for
AIGA Minnesota

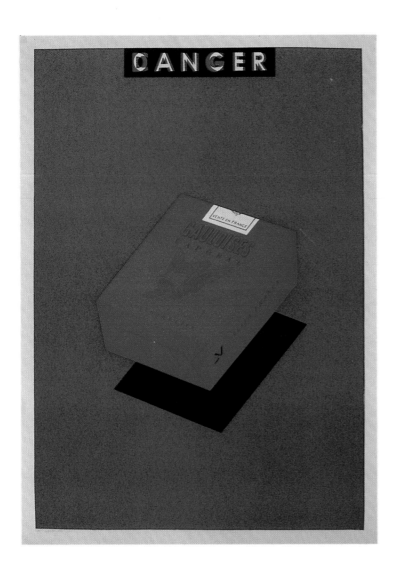

Designer
Alain Lequernec

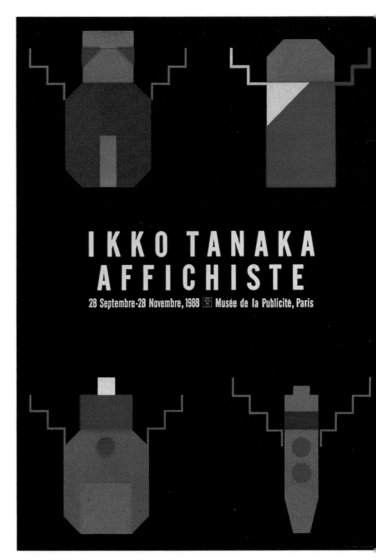

Designer
Ikko Tanaka
Description
Exhibition poster

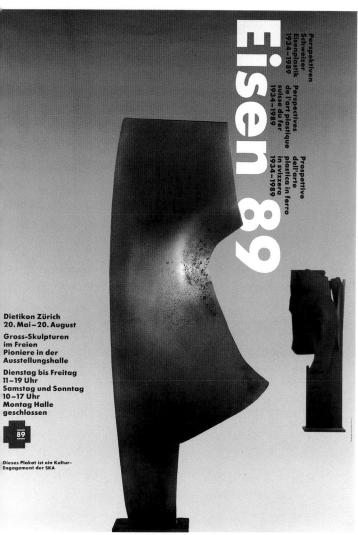

esigner
ritz Gottschalk
escription
wiss iron sculptures exhibition poster

Designer
Fritz Gottschalk
Description
Exhibition poster for Le Corbusier

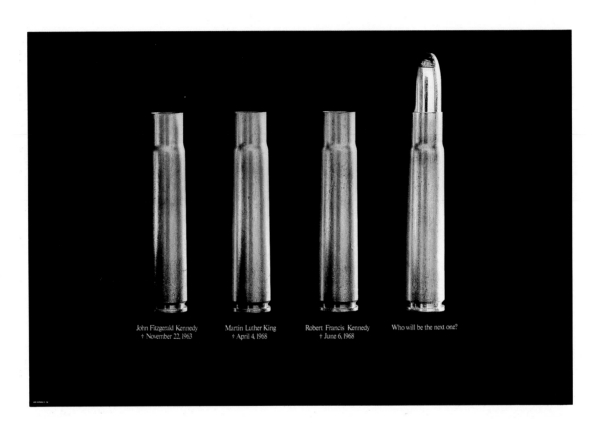

John Fitzgerald Kennedy
† November 22, 1963

Martin Luther King
† April 4, 1968

Robert Francis Kennedy
† June 6, 1968

Who will be the next one?

Designer
Erkki Ruuhinen

Designer
McRay Magleby
Description
Registration deadline pos

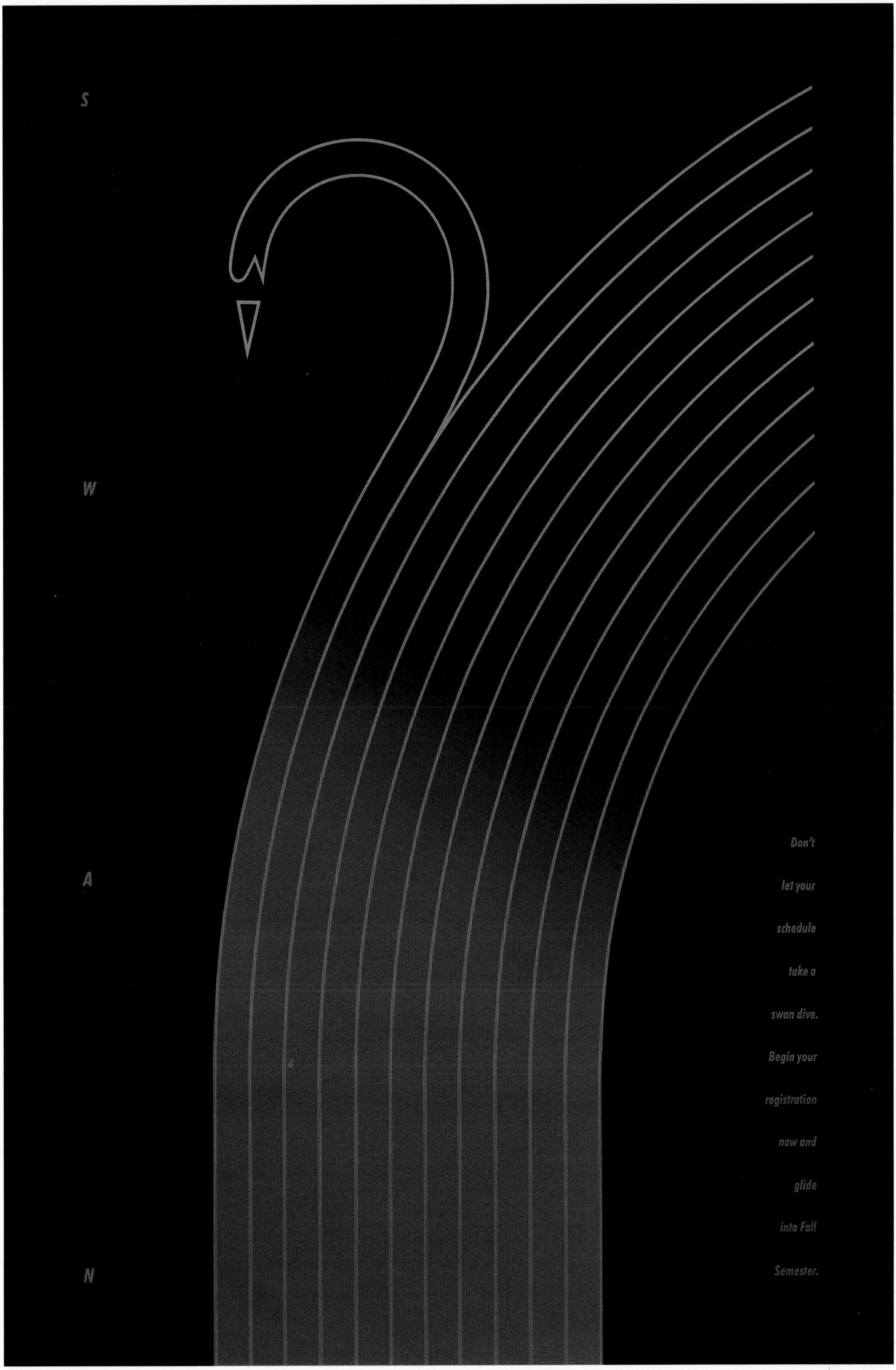

S

W

A

N

Don't

let your

schedule

take a

swan dive.

Begin your

registration

now and

glide

into Fall

Semester.

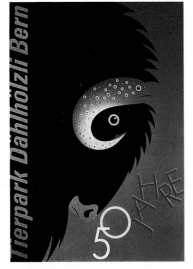

Designer
Niklaus Troxler
Client
Jazz in Willisau

Designer
Robert Krugel-Durband
Client
Radio Munsterton AG

Designer
Claude Kuhn-Klein
Client
Tierpark-Verein

Designer
Rolf Wenger
Client
Annabelle

Designer
Remy Fabrikant
Client
Mantel & Co.

Designer
Jorg Eigenmann
Client
Buchhandlung Comedia

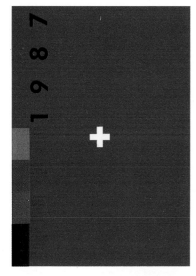

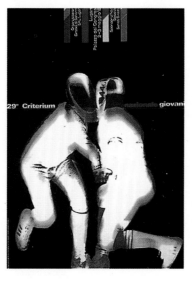

Designer
Odermatt + Tissi, Siegfried Odermatt
Client
Eidgenössisches Department
des Innern (EDI)

Designer
Paul Bruhwiler
Client
Filmpodium der Stadt Zürich

Designer
Dieter Hofmann
Client
Shell (Switzerland)

Designer
Bruno Monguzzi
Client
Circolo Scherma Sal

Designer
Werner Jeker
Client
Comité Officiel Le Corbusier
Musée des Beaux-Arts

Designer
Beate Keller
Client
Swiss Air and Coca Cola

Designer
Bülent Erkmen
Description
Pop concert poster

Designer
Bülent Erkmen
Description
Fashion show poster

Designer
Bülent Erkmen
Description
Championship post

X. Avrupa ve Akdeniz Okçuluk Şampiyonası
Xth European and Mediterranean Archery Championship
27 - 29 Haziran/June 1986, İzmir, TURKEY
TÜRKIYE OKÇULUK FEDERASYONU
TURKISH ARCHERY FEDERATION

Mudo'nun katkılarıyla gerçekleşmiştir *Thanks to the contributions of Mudo*

15

Designer
Mick Haggerty
Description
Album cover

Designer
Bo Bonfils
Description
Unpublished (gray version) and published
versions of a lithoposter for Fritz Hansen

BROOKS FOR WOMEN

Preserving the balance that nature built into your foot, your stride, and your sense of motion. Athletic Shoes for Women.

BROOKS FOR WOMEN

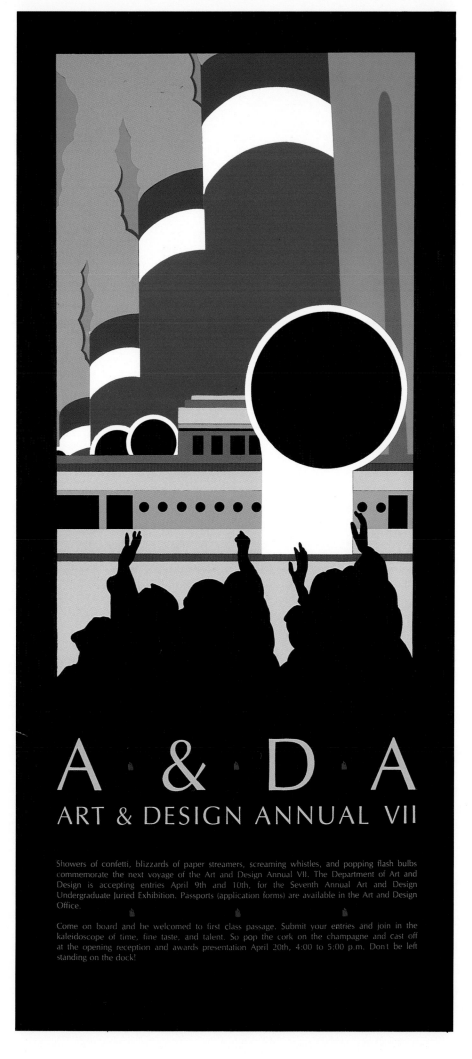

A & D A

ART & DESIGN ANNUAL VII

Showers of confetti, blizzards of paper streamers, screaming whistles, and popping flash bulbs commemorate the next voyage of the Art and Design Annual VII. The Department of Art and Design is accepting entries April 9th and 10th, for the Seventh Annual Art and Design Undergraduate Juried Exhibition. Passports (application forms) are available in the Art and Design Office.

Come on board and be welcomed to first class passage. Submit your entries and join in the kaleidoscope of time, fine taste, and talent. So pop the cork on the champagne and cast off at the opening reception and awards presentation April 20th, 4:00 to 5:00 p.m. Don t be left standing on the dock!

Designer
Alan Mickelson and Clint
Description
Exhibition poster

Designer
Charles S. Anderson
Description
Advertising poster

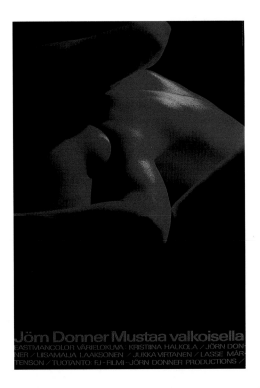

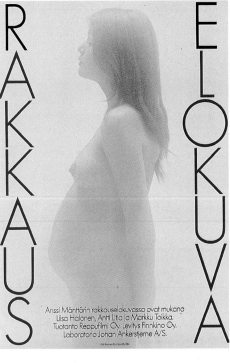

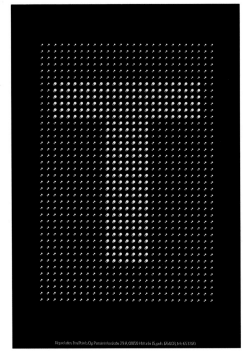

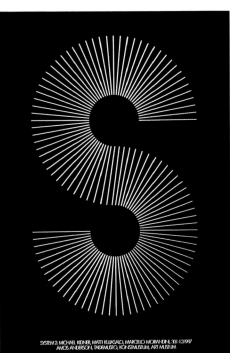

Designer
Erkki Ruuhinen
Description
Movie poster, poster for the Finnish Red Cross,
movie poster, poster, advertising poster, art
exhibition poster

A ESCOLA CULTURAL
NO ENSINO BÁSICO
E SECUNDÁRIO

SEMINÁRIO

COMISSÃO DE REFORMA DO
SISTEMA EDUCATIVO

27 E 28 DE MAIO DE 1987

UNIVERSIDADE DE TRÁS-OS-MONTES
E ALTO DOURO
VILA REAL

Designer
João Machado
Description
Announcing poster

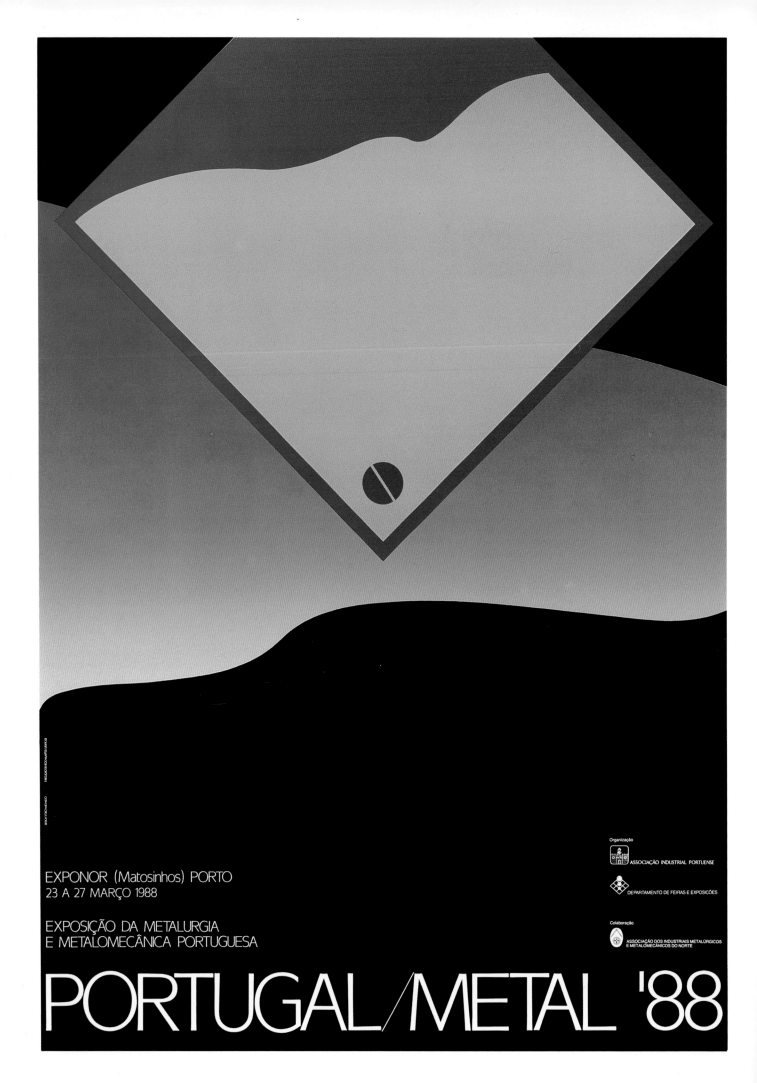

EXPONOR (Matosinhos) PORTO
23 A 27 MARÇO 1988

EXPOSIÇÃO DA METALURGIA
E METALOMECÂNICA PORTUGUESA

Organização
ASSOCIAÇÃO INDUSTRIAL PORTUENSE

DEPARTAMENTO DE FEIRAS E EXPOSIÇÕES

Colaboração
ASSOCIAÇÃO DOS INDUSTRIAIS METALÚRGICOS
E METALOMECÂNICOS DO NORTE

PORTUGAL/METAL '88

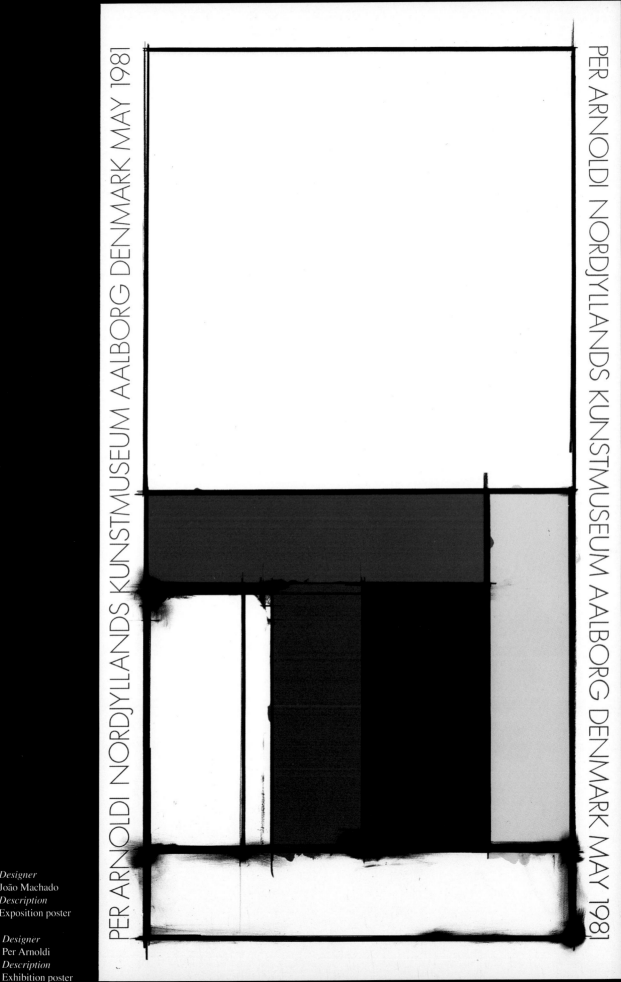

PER ARNOLDI NORDJYLLANDS KUNSTMUSEUM AALBORG DENMARK MAY 1981

PER ARNOLDI NORDJYLLANDS KUNSTMUSEUM AALBORG DENMARK MAY 1981

Designer
João Machado
Description
Exposition poster

Designer
Per Arnoldi
Description
Exhibition poster

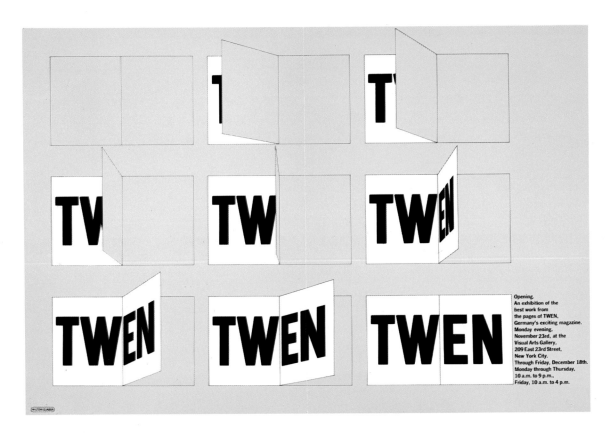

Opening.
An exhibition of the
best work from
the pages of TWEN,
Germany's exciting magazine.
Monday evening,
November 23rd, at the
Visual Arts Gallery,
209 East 23rd Street,
New York City.
Through Friday, December 18th.
Monday through Thursday,
10 a.m. to 9 p.m.,
Friday, 10 a.m. to 4 p.m.

Milanese Graphics
Tuesday evening
April 20th through
Tuesday, May 4th
The Visual Arts Gallery
209 East 23rd Street
New York City
Monday through
Thursday
10 a.m. to 9 p.m.
Friday 10 a.m.
to 4 p.m.

Designer
Milton Glaser
Art Director
Silas H. Rhodes
Description
Visual Arts Museum announcements

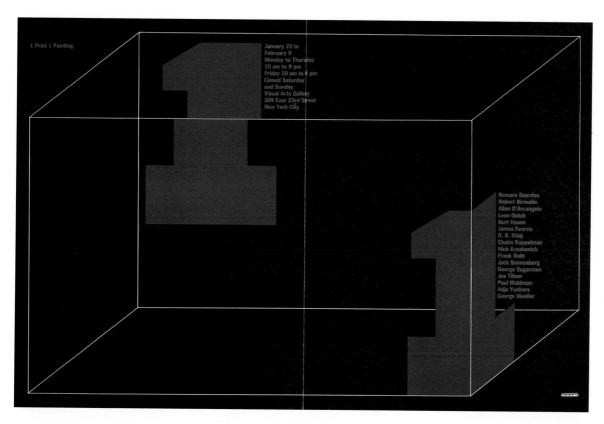

1 Print 1 Painting

January 23 to
February 9
Monday to Thursday
10 am to 9 pm
Friday 10 am to 4 pm
Closed Saturday
and Sunday
Visual Arts Gallery
209 East 23rd Street
New York City

Romare Bearden
Robert Birmelin
Allan D'Arcangelo
Leon Golub
Burt Hasen
James Kearns
R. B. Kitaj
Chaim Koppelman
Nick Krushenick
Frank Roth
Jack Sonnenberg
George Sugarman
Joe Tilson
Paul Waldman
Adja Yunkers
George Mueller

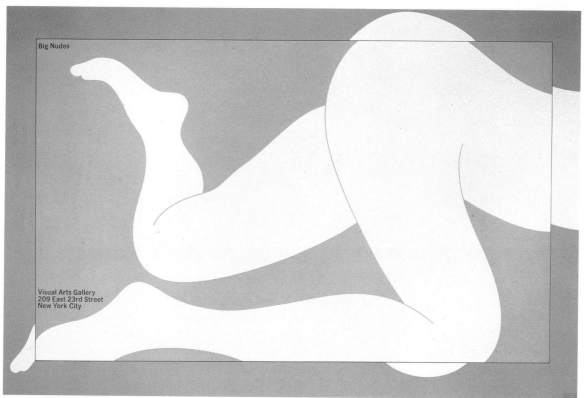

Big Nudes

Visual Arts Gallery
209 East 23rd Street
New York City

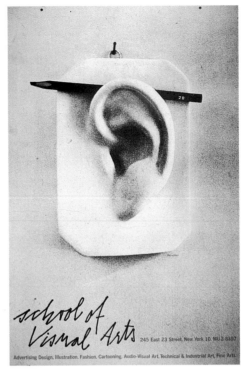

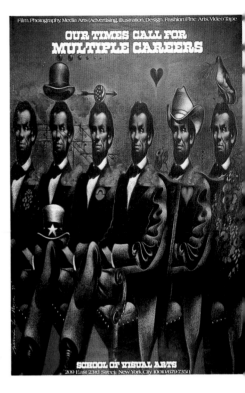

Designer
Bob Gill
Art Director
Silas H. Rhodes

Designer
Richard Wilde
Art Director
Silas H. Rhodes

Designer
Richard Wilde
Art Director
Silas H. Rhodes

Art Director
Silas H. Rhodes

Designer
George Tscherny
Art Director
Silas H. Rhodes

Designer
Sal de Vito
Art Director
Silas H. Rhodes

Department of Fine Arts: Painting, Drawing, Sculpture, Visual Perception, Printmaking
SCHOOL OF VISUAL ARTS
209 E. 23rd Street · New York, N.Y. 10010 · OR 9-7350 · Inquire: Office of Admissions

Technical
Illustration
Airbrush
Rendering
Photo
Retouching
School of
Visual Arts
209 E. 23 St.
New York 10010
OR 9-7350

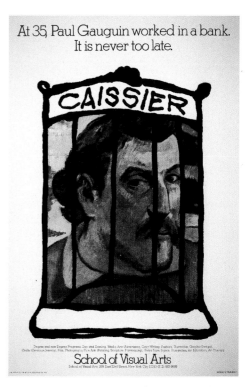

At 35, Paul Gauguin worked in a bank.
It is never too late.

CAISSIER

School of Visual Arts

To be good
is not enough,
when you
dream
of being great.

SCHOOL OF VISUAL ARTS

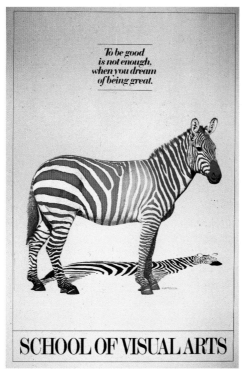

To be good
is not enough,
when you dream
of being great.

SCHOOL OF VISUAL ARTS

Designer
Milton Glaser
Art Director
Silas H. Rhodes

Designer
William J. Kobasz
Art Directors
Richard Wilde
Silas H. Rhodes

Designer
Paul Davis
Art Director
Silas H. Rhodes

Art Director
Gene Case

Designer
Ivan Chermayeff
Art Director
Silas H. Rhodes

Designer
Paula Scher
Art Director
Silas H. Rhodes

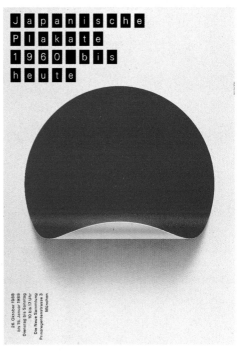

Designer
Mendell + Oberer
Description
Poster for the SOS children village

Designer
Mendell + Oberer
Description
Exhibition poster

Designer
Mendell + Oberer
Description
Flamenco dancer Antonio Gades

Designer
Mendell + Oberer
Description
Poster announcing renovation

Designer
Mendell + Oberer
Description
Exhibition poster

Designer
Mendell + Oberer
Description
Interior poster

Brigitta Hughes, Casting

Designer
Jayme Odgers
Art Director
Leslie Barnett
Description
Student Television Awards poster

 Los Angeles 1984 Olympic Games

April Greiman & Jayme Odgers   Copyright 1982 Los Angeles Olympic Organizing Committee   Published by Angeli Communications & Corporation

Designers
Jayme Odgers
April Greiman
Description
Games of the XXIII Olympiad

Polnische
Plakate

Polnische Plakate der
Nachkriegszeit

Ausstellung 4 der
Reihe »Zeugnisse« aus
den verborgenen Depots
der Neuen Sammlung

8. März bis 31. Mai 1986
Di bis So 10 bis 17 Uhr

Die Neue Sammlung
Staatliches Museum
für angewandte Kunst
Prinzregentenstraße 3
8000 München 22

Designer
Mendell + Oberer
Description
Sailing contest poster

Designer
Mendell + Oberer
Description
Exhibition poster

Deutsches Museum

| Bayerischer Staatspreis für Nachwuchs- designer 1988 | Bayerisches Staatsministerium für Wirtschaft und Verkehr | Ausstellung vom 22. März bis 24. April 1988 | Täglich geöffnet 9 bis 17 Uhr Museumsinsel 1 München |

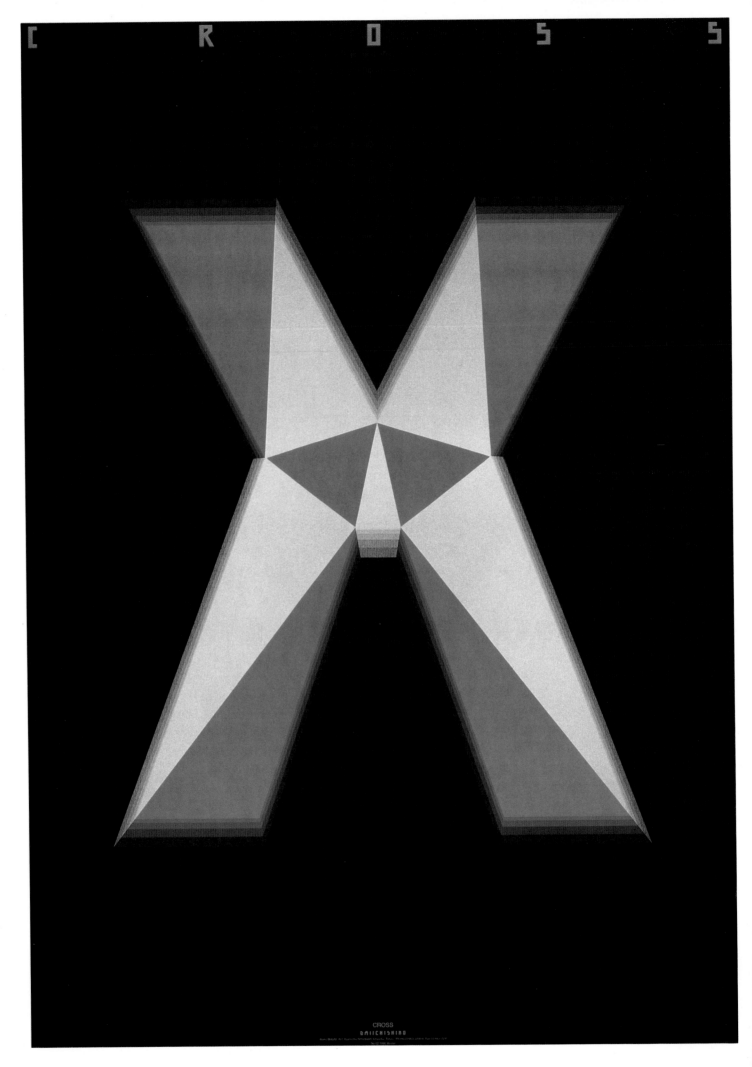

CROSS
DAIICHISHIRO

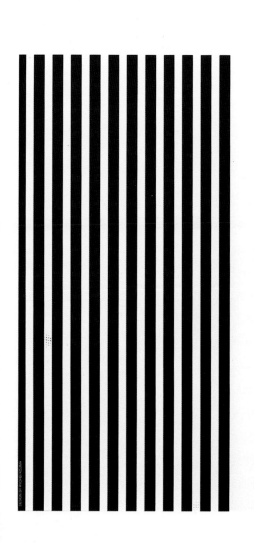

Designer
Y. Bokser
Description
The Cotton Club,
film poster

СТАЛИНИЗМ!
Ю. ЛЕОНОВ
(Москва).
III премия

Designer
V. Lebnov
Description
Stalinism, political poster

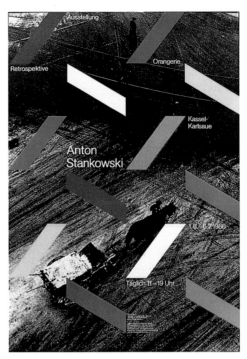

Designer
Gunter Rambow
Client
Egoist, Typographers

Designer
Gunter Rambow
Client
Cultural Ministry of Kassel

Designer
G. Rambow
Description
Exhibition poster, Anton Stankowski

Designer
Gunter Rambow
Title
International Spring Festival

Designer ▷
Gunter Rambow
Title
Classics of a somber time

Klassiker in finsteren Zeiten 1933-1945

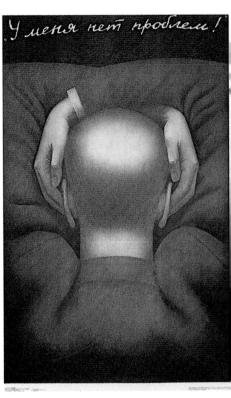

Designer
G. Ramkov
Description
Art poster

Designer
I. Tarasov
Description
Social poster

Designer
Unknown
Description
Sports poster

Designer
Y. Maystrovski
Description
Film poster

Designer
I. Lemeshev
Description
Political poster

Designer
A collaboration of many artists
Description
Film poster

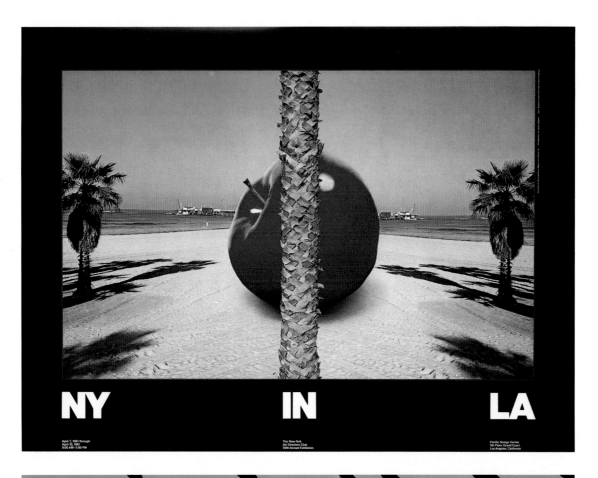

Designer
Jayme Odgers
Description
Poster for New York Art Directors Club show in
Los Angeles

Designer
Jayme Odgers
Description
On the road, personal work

Designer
McRay Magleby
Description
40th anniversary of the bombing of Hiroshima

Designer
Kyösti Varis
Description
Exhibition poster

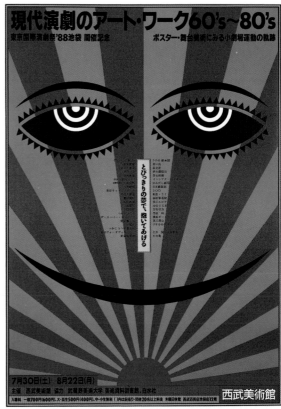

Designer
Shin Matsunaga
Description
Exhibition poster

Designer
Shin Matsunaga
Description
Exhibition poster

Designer
Shin Matsunaga
Description
Exhibition poster

Designer
Shin Matsunaga
Description
Poster for showroom of
Interior Equipment Company

Designer
Dan Reisinger
Description
Political poster

Designer
Dan Reisinger
Description
10th anniversary of the Diaspora Museum

Designer
Dan Reisinger
Description
Israel festival poster

Designer
Dan Reisinger
Title
Summer of '86

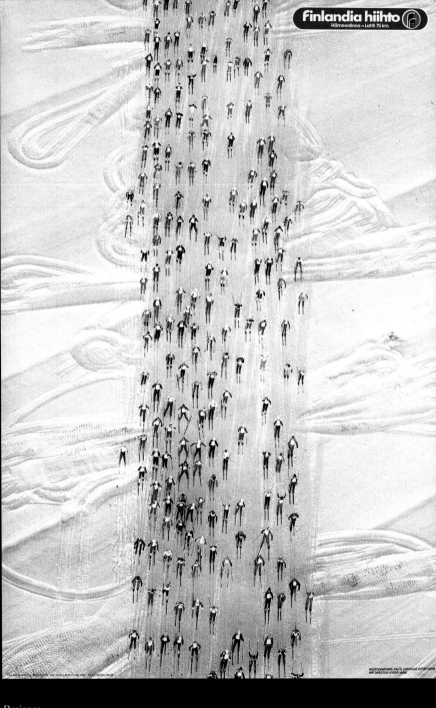

finlandia hiihto
Hämeenlinna → Lahti 75 km.

PHOTOGRAPHERS: KAJ G. LINDHOLM, KYÖSTI VARIS
ART DIRECTOR: KYÖSTI VARIS

Designer
Kyösti Varis
Description
Finlandia ski event

Designer
Kyösti Varis
Description
Newspaper advertisement

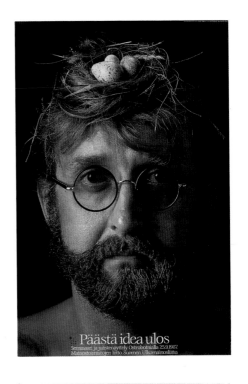

Designer
Kyösti Varis
Title
Let the idea out

Designer
Kyösti Varis
Description
Poster for Lahti
International Poster Biennale

Designer
Kyösti Varis
Title
Aids

Designer
Kyösti Varis
Title
Libris. Printers of good design

Designer
Kyösti Varis
Title
The cigarette cross

Designer
Kyösti Varis
Description
Finnish culture week in Poland

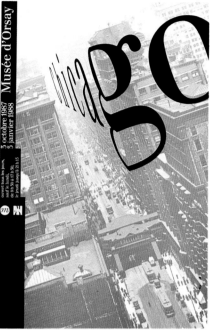

Designer
Pierre Bernard
Description
Exhibition poster

Designer
Pablo Feix
Client
The City of Montreail

Designer
Philippe Apeloig
Description
Exhibition poster

Designer
Claude Baillargeon
Client
Agency Infocom

Designer
Ronald Curchod
Client
The Lido, Townhall of Toulouse

Designer
Michel Bouvet
Client
The Theatre for Looking

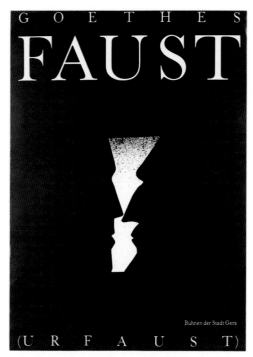

Designer
Klaus Ensikat
Description
Theatre poster

Designer
Erhard Grüttner
Description
Theatre poster

◁ *Designer*
Rolf Kuhrt
Description
Theatre poster for "Waiting For Godot"

Designer
Rolf Felix Müller
Description
Theatre poster

Designer
Volker Pfüller
Description
Theatre poster

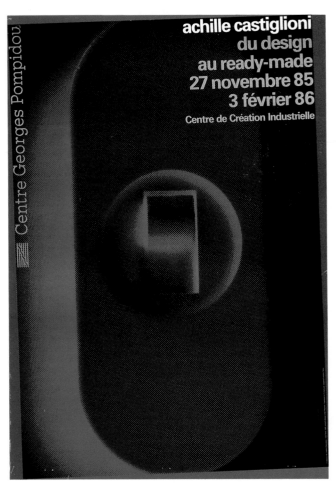

Designer
Jean Widmer
Description
Industrial design exhibition poster

Designer
Jean Widmer
Description
Photographic exhibition poster

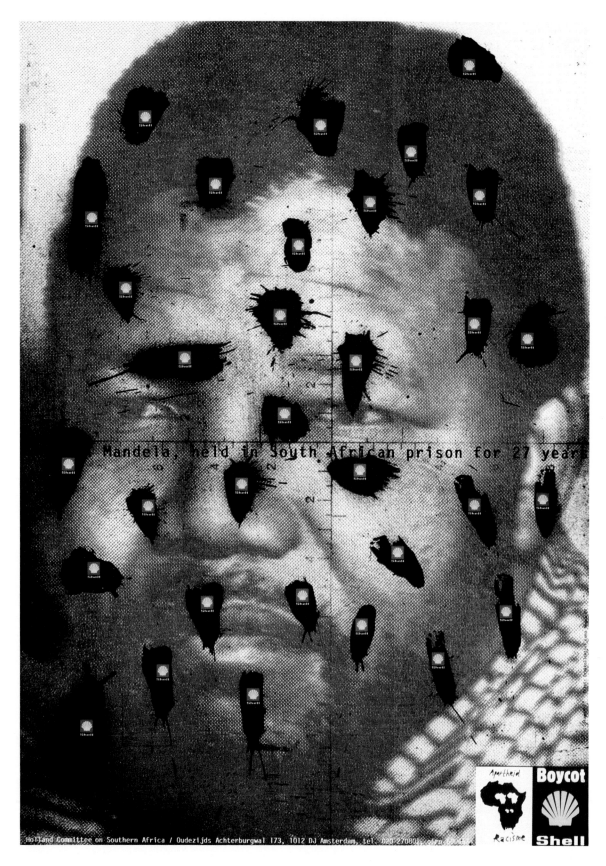

Designers
The Associated Graphic Designers
Description
Political poster

Designers
The Associated Graphic Designers
Description
Exhibition poster

FONDS D'ART MODERNE
ET CONTEMPORAIN

Espace Boris Vian - Parc des Ilets
Rue des Faucheroux 03100 MONTLUÇON

DE LA **VILLE DE MONTLUÇON**

Designer
Mariscal
Description
Exhibition poster

Designer
José Ortega
Title
Halley's comet

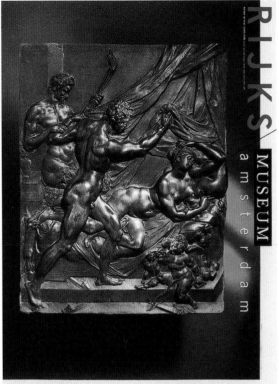

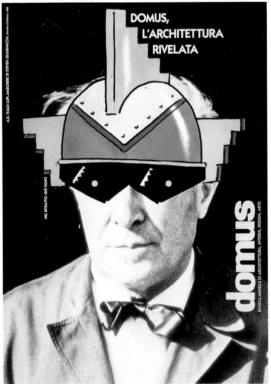

Designer
Eric Nuyten
Description
Exhibition poster

Designer
Italo Lupi
Description
Campaign for Domus Magazine

Designer
Saul Bass
Title
Human rights 1789 - 1989

Designer
Saul Bass
Description
Poster for the Los Angeles Film Exposition

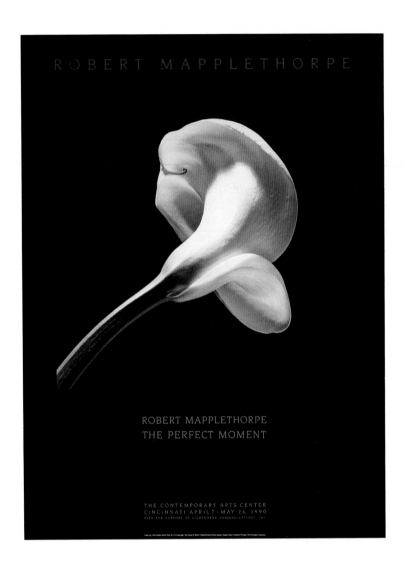

Designer
Julius Friedman
Description
Exhibition poster

Designers
Craig Frazier, Deborah Hagemann
Title
Men of letters

Designer
Wieslaw Walkask

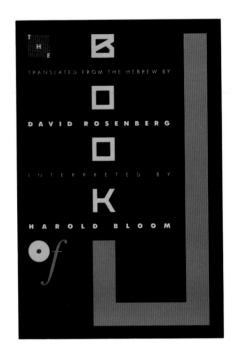

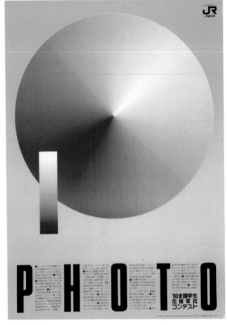

Designer
Carin Goldberg
Title
The book of J

Designer
Shuichi Nogami
Description
Flower Expo photo contest

Designer
Peter Steiner
Title
Poster self promotion - Quality

STICHTING OEUVRE + FRASCATI

sam shepard

festival

dinsdag 22.11
tot en met zaterdag 02.12.89

telefonisch reserveren (020) 26 68 66
aanvang voorstellingen: 20.00 uur

Designer
Keoweiden-Postma
Description
Festival poster

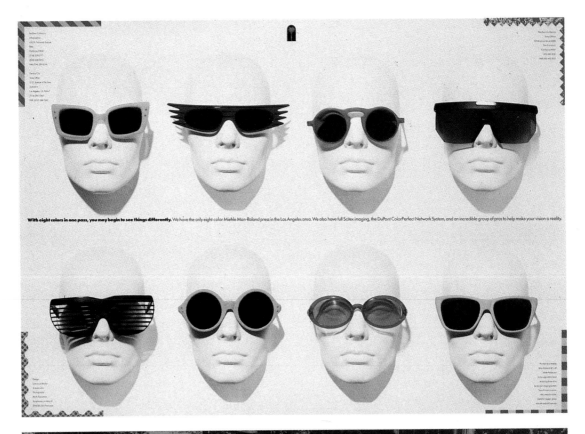

With eight colors in one pass, you may begin to see things differently. We have the only eight-color Miehle Man-Roland press in the Los Angeles area. We also have full Scitex imaging, the DuPont ColorPerfect Network System, and an incredible group of pros to help make your vision a reality.

Biggest ever. The third season of *The American Experience* tells great stories of people and places from our nation's history. Tune in Mondays at 9 p.m. beginning October 1 on public television. Made possible by Aetna.

Designers
Lawrence Bender, Timothy Lau
Title
Southern California lithograph

Designer
Peter Good
Title
The American Experience

Designer
Woody Pirtle
Title
From Start to Finish

Designer
Gim McMullan
Description
Theatre poster

Creative Director
Anthon Beeke
Illustrator
Kazimir Malevich
Description
Exhibition poster

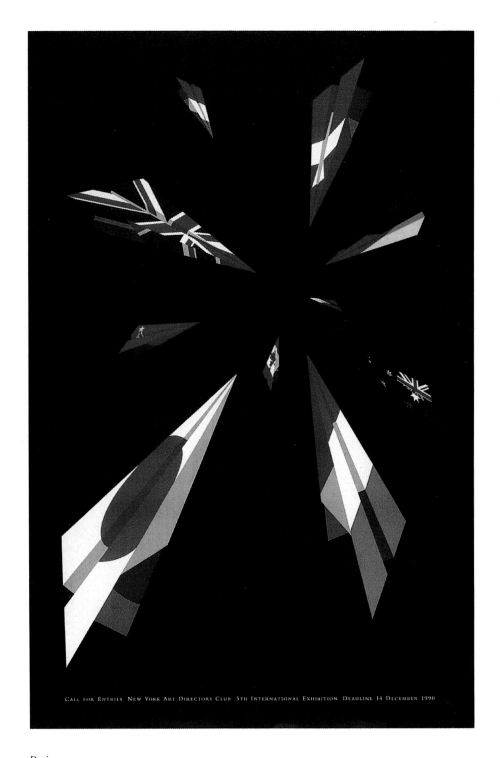

Designer
Michael Gericke
Description
Exhibition poster

Retur til
Kunsthåndverk
Kongensgt. 3
0153 Oslo 1
Pris kr. 50,-

H · Å · N · D · V · E · R · K

Retur til
Kunsthåndverk
Kongensgt. 3
0153 Oslo 1

Pris kr 50,-

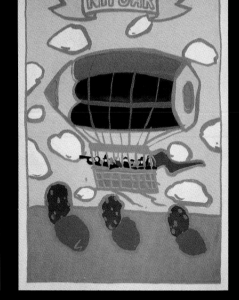

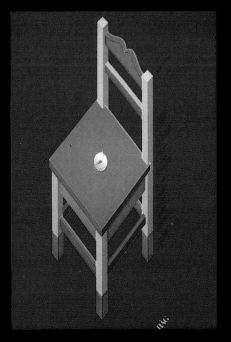

Designer
Bruno Oldani
Description
Film poster

Designer
Bruno Oldani

Client
Norsk Illustrator Forbund
Designer
Rolf Janson

Designer
Art Aid
Description

Designer
Michael Manwaring
Description
Poster for an AIGA event
on environmental concerns

Designer
Michael Manwaring
Description
Poster for the art directors and
artists club of Sacramento

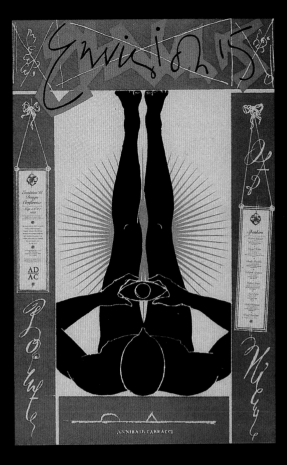

Art Director
McRay Magleby
Title
Skater

Client
York University
Designer
Victoria Primicias
Art Directors
Diti Katona, John Plypczak

Designer
Samuel Kuo
Art Directors
Samuel Kuo
Anthony Russel
Description
Join the Anthony Russell Fishing Party

Designer
Uwe Loesch
Description
Theatre poster

DAS KOM M ÖDCHEN *Leitung: Kay Lorentz*

DAS

Thomas Freitag, Jutta Hahn, Harald Schmidt

IST

Texte: Matthias Deutschmann, Wolfgang Franke,

IHR

Michail Krausnick, Harald Schmidt

PRO

Keyboards: Matthias Bröde *Bass:* Thomas Giesler

B

Drums: Peter Baumgärtner

E

Bühne: Pit Fischer

M

Regie: Kay Lorentz

!

Design: Uwe Loesch

Designer
Uwe Loesch
Description
Theatre poster

Designer ▷
Holger Matthies
Description
The 1991/92 season at the "Schauspiel Hannover"
(Hannover theatre), Germany

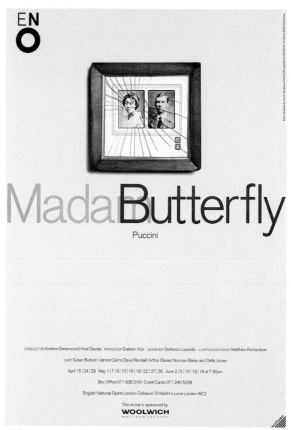

◁ *Designer*
Paris-Clavel
Description
Opening poster

Designers
Mike Dempsey, Barbo Ohlson
Description
Posters for the English National Opera

Designer
Mike Dempsey
Description
Poster for the BBC

Photo '93 is a compilation of over 300 images selected from a worldwide call for entries. □ **Graphis Typography 1** spans the years from the "founding fathers" of type design through the modern masters. A comprehensive time line, examples of computer aided type design and pictorial displays of past and present designers make this book invaluable. □ **Design '94** a classic Graphis annual with 700 examples of visual communication spanning 256 pages with such categories as design, illustration, advertising, brochures, letterheads and more. □ **Poster '93** contains over 400 images and 256 pages and features introductions by Ron Dumas: Creative Director/Graphic Designer of Nike footwear, Makoto Saito, Japanese poster illustrator and Catherine Bürer of the Swiss Poster Collection. □ **Graphis Nudes** with 224 pages and over 200 images, this book is an elegant and impressive collection of carefully

selected images by the world's outstanding photographers. □ **Graphis Annual Reports 4** features the best in annual report design from fiscal 1991 and 1992. These reports are selected based, not only on outstanding design style, but also for excellence in photography, illustration and over-all composition. □ **Letterhead 2** is suited to guide and inspire the graphic designer in creating strong visual identities. □ **Graphis Paper Specifier System (GPS)** includes cross referenced indexes organized by paper manufacturer and paper name, region of merchant directory and factual paper information. □ **Logo 2** extensive in scope, the book is packed with over 300 innovative top-quality logos, created for both large and small firms, as well as not-for-profit foundations and organizations. □ **Photo '93** ist eine Sammlung von über 300 Bildern, die auf Grund ihrer künstlerischen Qualität

anlässlich des neusten internationalen Graphis-Wettbewerbs ausgewählt wurden. □ **Graphis Typography 1** bietet ein breites Panorama der Schriftgestaltung, von den Anfängen der Typographie bis hin zu Schriften, die mit dem Computer entwickelt wurden. Eine zeitliche Übersicht führt von den «Gründervätern» zu den modernen Meistern, dokumentiert durch zahlreiche Abbildungen. □ **Design '94**, der Klassiker der Graphis-Jahrbücher, zeigt weit mehr als 700 Beispiele visueller Kommunikation (Gestaltung von Broschüren, Anzeigen, Zeitschriften, Briefköpfen etc.). 256 Seiten Design total. □ **Poster '93** enthält über 400 Bilder. Eingeleitet wird der 256 Seiten starke Band mit Texten von Ron Dumas, Creative Director/Graphic Designer für Nike-Schuhe, von Makoto Saito, dem japanischen Plakatkünstler, und von Catherine Bürer, Direktorin der

Plakatsammlung des Museums für Gestaltung, Zürich. □ **Graphis Nudes** versammelt auf 224 Seiten 200 sorgfältig ausgewählte Aktphotos von hervorragenden Photographen aus aller Welt. □ **Graphis Annual Reports 4** zeigt Jahresberichte für 1991 und 1992. Beurteilt wurde die Gestaltung, aber auch die Qualität von Illustrationen und Photographie sowie der Produktion. □ **Letterhead 2** bietet Anregung und Inspiration bei der Gestaltung ausserordentlicher visueller Erscheinungsbilder. □ **Graphis Paper Specifier System (GPS)** enthält Papiermuster sowie Indexe nach Herstellern und Papiersorten, Händlerverzeichnisse und Angaben zu den Papieren. □ **Logo 2** zeigt ein breites Spektrum von 300 innovativen, hervorragenden Logos für kleine und grosse Betriebe, Institutionen und Organisationen. □ **Photo '93** est un recueil

de plus de 300 illustrations choisies pour leur qualité artistique à l'occasion d'un concours international. □ **Graphis Typography 1** présente un panorama exhaustif du design typographique, des pionniers de l'ancienne génération aux plus grands créateurs actuels. Vous y trouverez aussi bien des exemples de typographies élaborées sur ordinateur que des créations de designers d'hier et d'aujourd'hui. □ **Design '94** présente plus de 700 exemples de communication visuelle (création de brochures, d'annonces, de publications, de papiers à entête etc.). □ **Poster '93** contient plus de 400 images. La préface de cet ouvrage de 256 pages est signée par Ron Dumas, directeur artistique et graphiste de la marque de chaussures Nike, Makoto Saito, le créateur d'affiches japonais, et par Catherine Bürer, conservatrice de la collection d'affiche du Museum für Gestaltung à Zurich. □ **Graphis**

Nudes rassemble sur 224 pages 200 des plus belles photos des grands photographes contemporains. □ **Graphis Annual Reports 4** présente le meilleur des rapports annuels de 1991 et 1992. Les rapports sont choisies essentiellement en fonction de leur composition, mais aussi pour leur valeur sur le plan de photo ou du dessin et leur qualité de production. □ **Letterhead 2** offre aux graphistes une source d'inspiration pour la création de fortes identités visuelles. □ **Graphis Paper Specifier System (GPS)** contient des échantillons de papier ainsi qu'un index des fabricants et des différentes variétés de papier, un annuaire des représentants ainsi que diverses informations. □ **Logo 2** présente un vaste éventail de 300 logos pleins d'innovation et de très haute qualité conçus pour les entreprises de toutes tailles ainsi que pour les organisations à but non-lucratif. □